That love is all
there is
is all we know of love.

— Emily Dickinson

Christmas 2001

To Loretta
I Love you
Lucy

Words of

LOVE

Poems & Quotations on the
Meaning of Love

Edited by
Susan Polis Schutz

Blue Mountain Press ®

Boulder, Colorado

Library of Congress Catalog Card Number: 99-32259
ISBN: 0-88396-521-6

ACKNOWLEDGMENTS appear on page 64.

▜ design on book cover is registered in the U.S. Patent and Trademark Office.

Manufactured in the United States of America
First Printing: June 1999

♻ This book is printed on recycled paper.

Library of Congress Cataloging-in-Publication Data

Words of love : poems & quotations on the meaning of love / edited by
    Susan Polis Schutz.
        p.   cm.
    ISBN 0-88396-521-6 (alk. paper)
    1. Love poetry. 2. Love Quotations, maxims, etc. I. Schutz, Susan Polis.
PN6110.L6W595 1999
808.81'93543--dc21   99-32259
                                                                                          CIP

Blue Mountain Press INC.

P.O. Box 4549, Boulder, Colorado 80306

CONTENTS

Love Is...

Love is
   being happy for the other person when they are happy
   being sad for the person when they are sad
   being together in good times
   and being together in bad times
Love is the source of strength

Love is
   being honest with yourself at all times
   being honest with the other person at all times
   telling, listening, respecting the truth
   and never pretending
Love is the source of reality

Love is
   an understanding that is so complete that
   you feel as if you are a part of the other person
   accepting the other person just the way they are
   and not trying to change them to be something else
Love is the source of unity

Love is
   the freedom to pursue your own desires
   while sharing your experiences with the other person
   the growth of one individual alongside of
   and together with the growth of another individual
Love is the source of success

Love is
    the excitement of planning things together
    the excitement of doing things together
Love is the source of the future

Love is
    the fury of the storm
    the calm in the rainbow
Love is the source of passion

Love is
    giving and taking in a daily situation
    being patient with each other's needs and desires
Love is the source of sharing

Love is
    knowing that the other person
    will always be with you regardless of what happens
    missing the other person when they are away
    but remaining near in heart at all times
Love is the source of security

Love is the
    source of life

                    — Susan Polis Schutz

It is the true season
of Love
When we know that
we alone can love,
that no one could ever
have loved before us
and that no one
will ever Love
in the same way
after us.

— Johann Wolfgang von Goethe

I love you
not as something private
and personal, which is my own,
but as something universal
and worthy of love
which I have found.

— Henry David Thoreau

Love consists in this
that two solitudes protect
and touch and greet
each other.

There is a miracle that happens every time to those
who really love: the more they give, the more they
possess of that precious nourishing love from which
flowers and children have their strength.

— Rainer Maria Rilke

When a Man and a Woman
Are in Love...

His life lies within hers
   and her life lies within his.
Each lives as an individual,
   yet they also live for one another;
each strives for independent goals,
   but they also work together
      to achieve their dreams.
When a man and a woman are in love,
   they will give to one another
      what they need to survive
      and help fulfill each other's wants.
They will turn one another's
   disappointment into satisfaction.
They will turn one another's
   frustration into contentment.
They will work as a mirror,
   reflecting to each other
      their strengths and weaknesses.
They will work together
   to alleviate the emotional walls
      that may separate them.
They will work together to build
   a better understanding of one another.
They will learn to lean on each other,
   but not so much as to be
      a burden on the other.

They will learn to reach out to one another,
    but not so much as to suffocate the other.
They will learn when it is time to speak
    and when it is time to listen.
They will be there to comfort each other
    in times of sorrow.
They will be there to celebrate together
    in times of happiness.
They will be one another's friend,
    guiding each other to the happiness
      that life holds.
They will be one another's companion,
    facing together the challenges
      that life may present.

When a man and a woman are in love,
    his life lies within hers
    and her life lies within his.
Together they will love one another
    for the rest of their lives
    and forever.
              — Stephen T. Fader

Nothing beats love. Love is the greatest healing power there is, nothing else comes close. Not ancient cures, modern medicines and technologies, or all the interesting books we read or the wise things we say and think. Love has a transformational power.

— Naomi Judd

Love does not consist
in gazing at each other,
but in looking outward
in the same direction.

— Antoine de Saint Exupéry

Love is at its best
    when it is given completely...

When you walk hand in hand
    with the person of your dreams
When you talk into the wee hours
        of the morning —
    sharing your most intimate thoughts
        and dreams
When you kiss each other's lips
    as delicately as the petals
        of the pinkest rose
When the darkest nights
    turn into the brightest mornings
        as you're held in each other's arms

When the tickle of a whisper in the ear
    is as warm as the breath of a fire
When you see endless color and passion
    in each other's eyes
When the sweetest embrace between you
    touches the depths of your souls

— Mark V. Marino

I Love You This Much...

Enough to do anything for you — give
　　my life, my love, my heart, and my
　　soul to you and for you.
Enough to willingly give all of my time,
　　efforts, thoughts, talents, trust, and
　　prayers to you.
Enough to want to protect you, care
　　for you, guide you, hold you, comfort
　　you, listen to you, and cry to you
　　and with you.
Enough to be completely comfortable
　　with you, act silly around you, never
　　have to hide anything from you, and
　　be myself with you.
Enough to share all of my sentiments,
　　dreams, goals, fears, hopes, and
　　worries — my entire life with you.
Enough to want the best for you, to
　　wish for your successes,
　　and to hope for the
　　fulfillment of all your
　　endeavors.

Enough to keep my promises to you
and pledge my loyalty and
faithfulness to you.
Enough to cherish your friendship,
adore your personality, respect your
values, and see you for who you are.
Enough to fight for you, compromise
for you, and sacrifice myself for you
if need be.
Enough to miss you incredibly when
we're apart, no matter what length of
time it's for and regardless of the
distance.
Enough to believe in our relationship, to
stand by it through the worst of
times, to have faith in our strength as
a couple, and to never give up on us.
Enough to spend the rest of my life
with you, be there for you when you
need or want me, and never, ever
want to leave you or live without you.

I love you this much.

— Lisa M. Thomas

A soul mate is someone to whom we feel profoundly connected, as though the communicating and communing that takes place between us were not the product of intentional efforts, but rather a divine grace. This kind of relationship is so important to the soul that many have said there is nothing more precious in life.

— Thomas Moore

Every soul is a celestial Venus to every other soul... Love is our highest word, and the synonym of God.

— Ralph Waldo Emerson

To My Soul Mate

Somehow, out of all the twists and turns our lives could have taken, and out of all the chances we might have missed, it almost seems like we were given a meant-to-be moment — to meet, to get to know each other, and to set the stage for a special togetherness.

When I am with you, I know that I am in the presence of someone who makes my life more complete than I ever dreamed it could be. I turn to you for trust, and you give it openly. I look to you for inspiration, for answers, and for encouragement, and — not only do you never let me down — you lift my spirits up and take my thoughts to places where my troubles seem so much further away and my joys feel like they're going to stay in my life forever.

I hope you'll stay forever, too. I feel like you're my soul mate. And I want you to know that my world is reassured by you, my tomorrows need to have you near, so many of my smiles depend on you, and my heart is so thankful that you're here.

— Carey Martin

By the accident of fortune a man
   may rule the world for a time,
but by virtue of love he
   may rule the world forever.

He who defends with love
   will be secure;
Heaven will save him, and
   protect him with love.

Kindness in words
   creates confidence.
Kindness in thinking
   creates profoundness
Kindness in feeling
   creates love.

— Lao Tzu

Take twin mounds of clay,
Mold them as you may.
Shape one after me,
Another after thee.
Then quickly break them both.
Remix, remake them both —
One formed after thee,
The other after me.

Part of my clay is thine;
Part of thy clay is mine.

— Kwan Tao-Shing
(13th Century)

Our love was pure
    as the snow on the mountains
White as a moon
    between the clouds.

— Cho Wen-Chun

PROMISES OF LOVE...

I promise you
my love,
For today
and tomorrow;
I promise you
as much happiness
as I can give;
I promise not
to doubt
or mistrust you,
But to grow
and add to your life
of content.
I promise
never to try to
change you,
But will accept
the changes you make
in yourself;
And I will accept
your love for me
without fear
of tomorrow;
knowing that
tomorrow,
I'll love you more
than I do today.

— Donna Pawluk

"I Love You" Is My Lasting Promise to You

Love is a word with many meanings.
So when I say, "I love you,"
I want you to understand exactly
   what I mean...

I don't say, "I love you"
   expecting something in return
or just to make you feel better.
I say it so that you know
   that no matter what else happens
      in your life,
there is at least one thing
   that you can count on:
                  me loving you.

I'll be there to
hold your hand in hard times,
calm you in distressed times,
and offer my help even when
   your pride may keep you
      from asking for it.

My love is unconditional,
   and it will always be there.
Even when everything else
   seems lost
and there is no hope in sight,
just remember one thing —
"I love you,"
and my love is genuine.

— Erica Denmark

Of all the creations
of the earth and heaven
love is the most precious.

Some say the most beautiful thing
on this dark earth
is a cavalry regiment,
some a battalion of infantry on the march,
and some a fleet of long oars.
But to me the fairest thing is when
one is in love with someone else.

— Sappho
(580 B.C.)

Shall I Compare Thee to a Summer's Day?

Shall I compare thee to a summer's day?
Thou art more lovely and more temperate:
Rough winds do shake the darling buds of May,
And summer's lease hath all too short a date:
Sometime too hot the eye of heaven shines,
And often in his gold complexion dimm'd;
And every fair from fair sometime declines,
By change or nature's changing course untrimm'd;
By thy eternal summer shall not fade
Nor lose possession of that fair thou owest;
Nor shall Death brag thou wander'st in his shade,
When in eternal lines to time thou growest;
So long as men can breathe or eyes can see,
So long lives this and this gives life to thee.

— William Shakespeare

WHEN MY LOVE'S AWAY...

Is the day better than the night?
Or is the night better than the day?
How can I tell?
But this I know is right:
Both are worth nothing
When my love's away.

— Amaru

Blow wind, to where my loved one is,
Touch him, and come and touch me soon:
I'll feel his gentle touch through you,
And meet his beauty in the moon.

These things are much for one who loves —
A person can live by them alone —
That he and I breathe the same air,
And that the earth we tread is one.

— Ramayana

With you there
and me here
I have had no one
to discuss little things with
like how the dew feels on the grass
or big things like
what's going on in the world

I have been lonely
talking and thinking to myself
I now realize how essential it is
to have someone
to share oneself with

— Susan Polis Schutz

Although I have a lamp and fire,
Stars, moon, and sun to give me light,
Unless I look into your eyes,
All is dark night.

— Bhartrhari

I keep thinking
about you
every few minutes
all day.

— Walt Whitman

Lighted Lamp

Love is something eternal — the aspect may change, but not the essence. There is the same difference in a person before and after he is in love as there is in an unlighted lamp and one that is burning. The lamp was there and it was a good lamp, but now it is shedding light, too, and that is its real function.

The best way to know life is to love many things.

— Vincent van Gogh

How do I love thee? Let me count the ways.
I love thee to the depth and breadth and height
My soul can reach, when feeling out of sight
For the ends of Being and ideal Grace.
I love thee to the level of everyday's
Most quiet need, by sun and candle-light.
I love thee freely, as men strive for Right;
I love thee purely, as they turn from Praise.
I love thee with the passion put to use
In my old griefs, and with my childhood's faith.
I love thee with a love I seemed to lose
With my lost saints, — I love thee with the breath,
Smiles, tears, of all my life! — and, if God choose,
I shall but love thee better after death.

— Elizabeth Barrett Browning

To My Dear and Loving Husband

If ever two were one, then surely we.
If ever man were loved by wife, then thee;
If ever wife was happy in a man,
Compare with me, ye women, if you can.
I prize thy love more than whole mines of gold
Or all the riches that the East doth hold.
My love is such that rivers cannot quench,
Nor ought but love from thee, give recompense.
Thy love is such I can no way repay,
The heavens reward thee manifold, I pray.
Then while we live, in love let's so persevere
That when we live no more, we may live ever.

— Anne Bradstreet

You are the person I am
always thinking of
You are the most important
person in the whole
world to me

You are the one I love

— Rebecca J. Barrett

I love you the more in that I believe
you have liked me for my
own sake and for nothing else.

— John Keats

You...
are something to me
between dream and miracle.

— Elizabeth Barrett Browning

My Delight and Thy Delight

My delight and thy delight
Walking, like two angels white,
In the gardens of the night:

My desire and thy desire
Twining to a tongue of fire,
Leaping live, and laughing higher;

Through the everlasting strife
In the mystery of life.

Love, from whom the world begun,
Hath the secret of the sun.
Love can tell, and love alone,
Whence the million stars were strewn,
Why each atom knows its own,
How, in spite of woe and death,
Gay is life, and sweet is breath:

This he taught us, this we knew,
Happy in his science true,
Hand in hand as we stood
'Neath the shadows of the wood,
Heart to heart as we lay
In the dawning of the day.

— Robert Bridges

My Love Is Come to Me

My heart is like a singing bird
Whose nest is in a water'd shoot;
My heart is like an apple tree
Whose boughs are bent with thick-set fruit;
My heart is like a rainbow shell
That paddles in a halcyon sea;
My heart is gladder than all these,
Because my love is come to me.
Raise me a dais of silk and down:
Hang it with fair and purple dyes;
Carve it in doves and pomegranates,
And peacocks with a hundred eyes;
Work it in gold and silver grapes,
In leaves and silver fleurs-de-lis;
Because the birthday of my life
Is come, my love is come to me.

— Christina Rossetti

YOU AND I

My hand is lonely for your clasping, dear;
   My ear is tired waiting for your call.
I want your strength to help, your laugh to cheer;
   Heart, soul and senses need you, one and all.
I droop without your full, frank sympathy;
   We ought to be together — you and I;
We want each other so, to comprehend
   The dream, the hope, things planned, or seen,
      or wrought.
Companion, comforter and guide and friend,
   As much as love asks love, does thought ask thought.
Life is so short, so fast the lone hours fly,
   We ought to be together, you and I.
                                    — Henry Alford

Wherever I am,
you are there
also.

— Ludwig van Beethoven

You know that
nothing can ever
change what we
have always been
and always will be
to each other.

— Franklin D. Roosevelt

Let us always
tell each other
our slightest griefs,
our smallest joys...
These confidences,
this exquisite intimacy,
are both the right
and the duty of love.

— Victor Hugo

LOVE IS NOT ALWAYS EASY,
BUT THERE'S NOTHING GREATER

When you're in love with someone, it doesn't mean that you are perfect in every way for each other. Sometimes certain personality traits may cause conflict in your relationship. You will always have your differences, but love encourages you not to despair. Being in love doesn't mean you won't make mistakes or you won't hurt each other. It doesn't mean that you will always think alike. Sometimes you hurt the ones you love the most because you take them for granted. They see all sides of you, not just the well-groomed, controlled side you present to others less familiar.

Sometimes pride clouds your vision and may keep you from using good judgment, making responsible decisions, and practicing forgiveness. But love will get you over the walls. It will bring you to your senses and provide balance and security if you allow it to. There's nothing like the satisfaction you feel when you're settled in the heavens of love's glory. It's worth the wait. It's worth the price you pay. It may not always be easy, but there's nothing greater than love.

— Donna Fargo

In order to have
   a successful relationship
you need to put out of your mind
any lessons learned
   from previous relationships
because if you carry
   a sensitivity or fear with you
you won't be acting freely
and you won't let yourself
   be really known

In order to have
   a successful relationship
it is essential that both people
be completely open and honest

— Susan Polis Schutz

A true relationship
knows of but one great thing:
   to give of one's self boundlessly
   in order to find one's self
   richer, deeper, better.

— Emma Goldman

There is no difficulty that enough love
will not conquer; No disease that enough love
will not heal; No door that enough love
will not open; No gulf that enough love
will not bridge; No wall that enough love
will not throw down; No sin that enough love
will not redeem...

It makes no difference how deeply seated
may be the trouble,
How hopeless the outlook,
How muddled the tangle,
How great the mistake, —
A sufficient realization of love will dissolve
it all... If only you could love enough,
you would be the happiest and most powerful
being in the world.

— Emmet Fox

Love is all we have; the only way
that each can help the other.

— Euripides

To renounce your individuality,
>to see with another's eyes,
>to hear with another's ears,
To be two and yet one,
>to so melt and mingle
>that you no longer know
>you are you or another,
To constantly absorb and
>constantly radiate,
To reduce earth, sea and sky
>and all that in them is
>to a single being so wholly
>that nothing whatever is withheld,
To be prepared at any moment
>for sacrifice,
To double your personality
>in bestowing it —
>that is love.

— Theophile Gautier

Love suffers long and is kind;
love does not envy;
love does not parade itself,
is not puffed up;
does not behave rudely,
does not seek its own,
is not provoked, thinks no evil;
does not rejoice in iniquity,
but rejoices in the truth;
bears all things, believes all things,
hopes all things, endures all things.

Love never fails.

— 1 Corinthians 13:4-8 (NKJV)

Let us not love in word or in
tongue, but in deed and in truth.

— 1 John 3:18 (NKJV)

When You Love Someone...

When you love someone,
you can't give too much more
        than yourself.
You can admit when
        you're wrong.
You never hesitate to say
        "I'm sorry."
You're always there to listen
and to lend a helping hand.

When you love someone,
you make sacrifices —
        no matter how great.
You know that in this person
all your dreams can be found.
You begin to believe
        not only in yourself,
but in another, as well.

When you love someone,
you don't take anything for granted.
You remember every smile, every kiss,
and every "I love you."

This person makes you happier
than you've ever been —
someone who is not only your love,
but also your best friend.

— Jennifer Brooks

To Love Someone Is Life's Greatest Gift

To love someone
   is to experience every other emotion outside of love
   and still come back to love.

To love someone
   is to feel hurt or pain and be able to overcome it
   and to forget about it.

To love someone
   is to realize that the other person is not perfect. It is
   being able to see their bad parts, but put emphasis on
   the parts you love, and gladly accept them for the
   individual they are.

To love someone
   is to lay a strong base for your feelings, but leave room
   for some fluctuation, because to feel exactly the same
   way all the time would leave no room for growth,
   experience, and learning.

To love someone
   is to be strong in accepting new ideas and facts. It is
   knowing that a person will not stay the same, but also
   that change happens gradually.

To love someone
   is to give until your heart aches. The greatest gifts
   shared between two people are trust and understanding,
   which come from love. Love is giving one hundred and
   ten percent of yourself and only wanting something as
   simple as a smile in return.

To love someone
   is to be able to see not only with your eyes but with
   your heart. It is to develop insight into your feelings
   and the other person's feelings, and have a good
   understanding of your relationship.

To love someone
   is to give of yourself totally, saying, "Here I am, and all
   that I am loves you very much." It is not twisting and
   turning and changing yourself to gain approval, but it is
   improving yourself so that your good points catch the
   other's attention and overshadow your faults.

   — Teresa M. Reiches

All that we are
is the result of what we think.

How then can a man escape being filled with hatred,
if his mind is constantly repeating... He misused me,
he hit me, he defeated me, he robbed me — ?

Hatred can never put an end to hatred;
hate is conquered only by love.

— Buddha

Time Is...

Too Slow for those who Wait,
Too Swift for those who Fear,
Too Long for those who Grieve,
Too Short for those who Rejoice;

But for those who Love,
Time is Eternity.

— Henry van Dyke

Whoever lives true life, will love true love.

— Elizabeth Barrett Browning

That love is all
there is
is all we know of love.

— Emily Dickinson

Love is... the joy of the good, the wonder
of the wise, the amazement of the gods.

— Plato

To love
means to communicate
    to the other
that you are all for him,
that you will never fail him
or let him down
when he needs you,
but that you
will always
be standing by.

— Ashley Montagu

There is nothing more
    wonderful in the world
than the feeling
    you get from sharing,
and there is no
    greater happiness
than the warmth
    you get from loving.

— J. Russell Morrison

I wish I could make you
understand how I love you.
I am always seeking, but
    cannot find a way...

I love in you a something
that only I have discovered —
the you — which is beyond the
    you of the world that is
    admired and known by others;
a "you" which is especially mine;
which cannot ever change,
and which I cannot ever
    cease to love.

— Guy de Maupassant

I want not only to be loved,
But to be told that I am loved.

— George Eliot

I Love You

I love you,
Not only for what you are
But for what I am
When I am with you.

I love you
Not only for what
You have made of yourself
But for what
You are making of me.

I love you
For the part of me
That you bring out;
I love you
For putting your hand
Into my heaped-up heart
And passing over
All the foolish, weak things
That you can't help
Dimly seeing there,
And for drawing out
Into the light
All the beautiful belongings
That no one else had looked
Quite far enough to find.

I love you because you
Are helping me to make
Of the lumber of my life
Not a tavern
But a temple;
Out of works
Of my every day
Not a reproach
But a song.

I love you
Because you have done
More than any creed
Could have done
To make me good,
And more than any fate
Could have done
To make me happy.

You have done it
Without a touch,
Without a word,
Without a sign.

You have done it
By being yourself.
Perhaps that is what
Being a friend means,
After all.

   — Roy Croft

Love does not dominate;
it cultivates.

Love has power to give in a
moment what toil can scarcely
reach in an age.

I am so glad that you are here
it helps me to realize how
beautiful my world is.

— Johann Wolfgang von Goethe

Nature produces
the greatest results
with the simplest
means. These are
simply the sun,
flowers,
water,
and
love.

— Heinrich Heine

If all the world were mine to plunder
I'd be content with just one town,
And in that town, one house alone,
And in that house, one single room,
And in that room, one cot only,
For there, asleep, is the one I love.

— Ancient Sanskrit Poem

Of all earthly music, that which
reaches the farthest into heaven
is the beating of a loving heart.

Love is the river of life in this world. Think
not that ye know it who stand at the little
tinkling rill, the first small fountain.

Not until you have gone through the rocky
gorges, and not lost the stream; not until
you have gone through the meadow, and
the stream has widened and deepened until
fleets could ride on its bosom; not until
beyond the meadow you have come to the
unfathomable ocean, and poured your
treasures into its depths — not until then
can you know what love is.

— Henry Ward Beecher

Some Things I Love

Your enchantment in a lonely wood,
The fight and color of a rainbow trout,
My in-basket empty and a good new book,
Binoculars fixed on a strange new bird,
Sadie's point, and a covey of quail,
The end of a six-mile run in the rain,
Blue slope, soft snow, fast run, no fall,
A dovetail joint without a gap,
Grandchildren coming in our front door,
The same ones leaving in a day or two,
And life, till what rhymes best with breath
takes me from all things I share with you.

— Jimmy Carter

It is a good thing to be
rich and to be strong,
but it is a better thing
to be loved.
— Euripides

Outside are the storms and strangers: we —
Oh, close, safe, warm sleep I and she,
— I and she!

Chance cannot change my love,
nor time impair.

What's the earth
With all its art, verse, music, worth
Compared with love, found, gained and kept?

— Robert Browning

Be My Friend,
My Partner, My Love...

Be my friend before all else.
Share laughter and smiles with me.
I want to exchange ideas, thoughts,
   and opinions with you.
I want to be able to confide in you,
   and have you confide in me.

Be my partner,
so that I may share my life,
   my love, my spiritual growth.
I want to build my hopes
   and dreams with you.
I want to begin each day with you
   and end each day the same way.

Be my love,
so that I may hold you,
   touch you,
give my heart to you,
   and share my soul.
Be my friend, my partner,
   my love.

— Linda Bray

The World Is Not
a Pleasant Place to Be

the world is not a pleasant place
to be without
someone to hold and be held by

a river would stop
its flow if only
a stream were there
to receive it

an ocean would never laugh
if clouds weren't there
to kiss her tears

the world is not
a pleasant place to be without
someone

— Nikki Giovanni
(17 feb 72)

When someone cares
   it is easier to speak
   it is easier to listen
   it is easier to play
   it is easier to work

When someone cares
   it is easier to laugh

— Susan Polis Schutz

The thing that counts most
in the pursuit of happiness
is choosing
the right traveling companion.

— Adrian Anderson

Once I knew the depth where no hope was and darkness lay on the face of all things. Then love came and set my soul free. Once I fretted and beat myself against the wall that shut me in. My life was without a past or future, and death a consummation devoutly to be wished. But a little word from the fingers of another fell into my hands that clutched at emptiness, and my heart leaped up with the rapture of living. I do not know the meaning of darkness, but I have learned the overcoming of it.

— Helen Keller

All, everything that I understand,
I understand only because I love.

— Leo Tolstoy

Ashes of Life

Love has gone and left me and the days are all alike;
Eat I must, and sleep I will, — and would that night
   were here!
But ah! — to lie awake and hear the slow hours strike!
Would that it were day again! — with twilight near!

Love has gone and left me and I don't know what to do;
This or that or what you will is all the same to me;
But all the things that I begin I leave before I'm through, —
There's little use in anything as far as I can see.

Love has gone and left me, — and the neighbours knock
   and borrow,
And life goes on forever like the gnawing of a mouse, —
And tomorrow and tomorrow and tomorrow and
   tomorrow
There's this little street and this little house.

— Edna St. Vincent Millay

Love

Love... a small word for such a complex emotion. There is no simple explanation for it, because love is made up of many things. It cannot be measured, because it is a feeling.

All of the money in the world cannot buy love; it has to be earned. It does not happen by wishing; it must come about naturally.

Love is not an instantaneous emotion, but something that grows slowly between two people, maturing with time. Once love has reached maturity, there is no stronger bond between two people.

To love someone means being comfortable and at ease with them, sharing confidences knowing that they will be understood and held in trust. It means respecting each other's dignity and never being demanding, but rather being willing to give, and accepting that which is given, graciously and with love.

To love someone means having a genuine concern for them, being able to sense that something is wrong without being told. It is understanding the other person's problems, moods, and "hang-ups," and accepting all of them even if you don't quite understand. It is excusing their faults, because you know that their good points far outweigh the bad.

Love is always being there for each other with a shoulder to cry on, to give support when confidence levels are low, to give helpful advice when it is asked for, to know when to be silent and just listen, or to give cheerful words of encouragement.

Love is sharing the good and the bad, the hopes and the dreams, the amusing times and the serious times. It is doing things together, yet leaving room for each to grow as an individual.

How do I know these things about love? Because this is the kind of love you have given to me and the kind of love I feel for you.

I am blessed with your love, and I will never take it for granted. I will strive to become an even better person and to always be deserving of your love, because I truly love you as I have never loved before.

— Beverly Bruce

The love you seek is seeking you at this moment. Your longing, your deep fantasies about being loved are mere shadows of the melting sweetness that makes spirit want to love you. Be honest about your seeking, and be alert to the moments when love is showing itself to you. You are the only means that love has for conquering its opposition; therefore you are infinitely precious in the eyes of spirit. The messages of love may not be clear to anyone else around you, even those most intimate to you. That doesn't matter; they are meant for you and you alone. Be assured of that.

— Deepak Chopra

One who walks
a road with love
will never
walk the road
alone.

— C. T. Davis

The Miracle of Love

Love doesn't mean that you will never feel pain or live a life free from care. It doesn't mean that you will never be hurt or that your life will be perfect, with every moment consumed by happiness.

Love does mean that you will always have a companion, someone to help you through the difficult times and rejoice with you in your times of celebration. Love does mean that each argument is followed by a time of forgiveness, and each time of sorrow is far outweighed by all the tender moments spent in each other's arms.

Love is the miracle that can take two lives and mold them into one, take two souls and bind them for life, take two hearts and fill them with enough passion and tenderness to last a lifetime.

Love is a blessing that will lead you down life's most beautiful path.

— Michele Weber

I Love You
More Than "Love"

It is impossible to capture in words
the feelings I have for you
They are the strongest feelings that I
have ever had about anything
yet when I try to tell you them
or try to write them to you
the words do not even begin to touch
the depths of my feelings
And though I cannot explain the essence of
these phenomenal feelings
I can tell you what I feel like
    when I am with you
When I am with you it is as if
    I were a bird
        flying freely in the clear blue sky

When I am with you it is as if
    I were a flower
        opening up my petals of life
When I am with you it is as if
    I were the waves of the ocean
        crashing strongly against the shore
When I am with you it is as if
    I were the rainbow after the storm
        proudly showing my colors
When I am with you it is as if
    everything that is beautiful
        surrounds us
This is just a very small part of how wonderful
I feel when I am with you
Maybe the word "love" was invented to explain
the deep, all-encompassing feelings
    that I have for you
but somehow it is not strong enough
But since it is the best word that there is
let me tell you a thousand times that
I love you more than
"love"

— Susan Polis Schutz

ACKNOWLEDGMENTS

We gratefully acknowledge the permission granted by the following authors, publishers, and authors' representatives to reprint poems or excerpts from their publications.

Scripture quotations in this publication are from the New King James Version. Copyright © 1979, 1980, 1982 by Thomas Nelson, Inc. All rights reserved. Reprinted by permission.

Villard Books, a division of Random House, Inc. for "Nothing beats love...." from LOVE CAN BUILD A BRIDGE by Naomi Judd with Bud Schaetzle. Copyright © 1993 by Naomi Judd. All rights reserved. Reprinted by permission.

Jennifer Brooks for "When You Love Someone...." Copyright © 1999 by Jennifer Brooks. All rights reserved. Reprinted by permission.

HarperCollins Publishers, Inc. for "A soul mate is someone..." from SOUL MATES by Thomas Moore. Copyright © 1994 by Thomas Moore. All rights reserved. Reprinted by permission.

Linda Bray for "Be My Friend, My Partner, My Love...." Copyright © 1999 by Linda Bray. All rights reserved. Reprinted by permission.

William Morrow & Company, Inc. for "The World Is Not a Pleasant Place to Be" from MY HOUSE by Nikki Giovanni. Copyright © 1972 by Nikki Giovanni. All rights reserved. Reprinted by permission.

Times Books, a division of Random House, Inc. for "Some Things I Love" from ALWAYS A RECKONING, AND OTHER POEMS by Jimmy Carter. Copyright © 1995 by Jimmy Carter. All rights reserved. Reprinted by permission.

Elizabeth Barnett, literary executor, for "Ashes of Life" by Edna St. Vincent Millay. From COLLECTED POEMS, HarperCollins. Copyright © 1917, 1923, 1945, 1951 by Edna St. Vincent Millay and Norma Millay Ellis. All rights reserved. Reprinted by permission.

Crown Publishers, Inc. for "The love you seek..." from THE PATH TO LOVE by Deepak Chopra. Copyright © 1997 by Deepak Chopra, M.D. All rights reserved. Reprinted by permission.

A careful effort has been made to trace the ownership of poems and excerpts used in this anthology in order to obtain permission to reprint copyrighted materials and give proper credit to the copyright owners. If any error or omission has occurred, it is completely inadvertent, and we would like to make corrections in future editions provided that written notification is made to the publisher:

BLUE MOUNTAIN PRESS, INC., P.O. Box 4549, Boulder, Colorado 80306.